Welcome to
Guardian Angel School

Poems by

Jody Winer

Finishing Line Press
Georgetown, Kentucky

Write down: I don't know.

—Wislawa Szymborska

Welcome to Guardian Angel School

*For my family
and
my family of friends*

Copyright ©2020 by Jody Winer
ISBN 978-1-64662-141-5 First Edition
All rights reserved under International and Pan-American Copyright Conventions. No part of this book may be reproduced in any manner whatsoever without written permission from the publisher, except in the case of brief quotations embodied in critical articles and reviews.

Publisher: Leah Maines

Editor: Christen Kincaid

Cover Photo: Jody Winer

Author Photo: Karen Robbins

Cover Design: Anita Merk

Printed in the USA on acid-free paper.
Order online: www.finishinglinepress.com
        also available on amazon.com

                Author inquiries and mail orders:
                      Finishing Line Press
                      P. O. Box 1626
                Georgetown, Kentucky 40324
                          USA

Contents

I.

The Creature Grief	1
Geography	2
Welcome to Guardian Angel School	3
Divisible	4
The Boys	5
My Little Planet	6
How to Arrive at a Motel	7
The Maréchal de Mouchy Departs a Funeral	8
Accident	9
After Halloween	10
Burnt Orchard	11
Another Art	12
Next	13
Revival	14

II.

Oh	17
Bed	18
Bodice Ripper	19
You Can Know How to Swim & Still Drown	20
Mrs. Sherlock Holmes States Her Case	21
House of Smoke	23
High Dive	24
The Lovers	25
Ferns, Lichens, Liverworts, etc.	26
Courtship Behavior of the Alligator	27
All Vermeer	28
The Button Master's Apprentice	29
Light	30
In Case You Misunderstood	31

I.

The Creature Grief

       He makes you write
your dead friend's name on the grocery list.
      You know him
by his sticky little tentacles
       treacle slipping from his lips
as he offers an embrace and one by one
      six thin arms grip you and not hands
but suction cups palpate your body as if
      marking property. He claims you in sun
though he prefers rainy days when water fills
      downspouts without restraint.
He is cloud and traffic light
      and pain-killer aisle at Rite-Aid
as he moves smoothly through your neighborhood.
      He sips coffee on a park bench
or behind the register at the coffee shop he demands
      all your cash. He is bigger than you
will ever be and sits on you when he wants
      his plump rump against your chest
your lungs struggling to breathe.

Geography
    (After W.S. Merwin)

If we had not bombed Cambodia I would not
have been standing over the heating grate
at 116th Street and Broadway selling roasted chestnuts
for the Quakers and the stone-hearted geology student
I eventually married would not have paused
to advise me that the sidewalk was shale and
if my great-grandmother had not danced for the Tsar
and my grandfather had not been mesmerized
by my grandmother's huge heart-shaped amethyst
mined most likely by Siberian slaves
then my mother would not have dropped
one oar at dusk into Lake Ardor and
the night swimmer who was to become my father
would not have heard her cries and if the German
baby nurse had not pulled my fingers
from my mouth or kept me from eating dust
I would not have sent away for an ant farm
or been haunted by the story of the freed Virginia slave
returned to captivity and I would not have become
an expert on plants that grow in saltwater
or embarked on a cross-country macrobiotic diet
in a 1954 Ford with a man I had known
only two days arriving in Miami just in time
to spend New Year's Eve breathing old ammonia
and holding my father's hand so dry
there was no sweat left while the ball
slipped slowly in Times Square and morphine
dripped from a glass bottle glistening
like grandmother's finest crystal.

Welcome to Guardian Angel School

Can I stop a dog from gnawing its tail?
you ask. *Save a child from blindness? Rescue
a meadow?* You want to understand your
range of motion. You will face rogue rivers,
scheming mosquitoes, rice shortages. Not
to mention surgeons with unsteady hands.
Check behind bedroom doors. Never ignore
leaky boats, uneasy seas. Yes, prayer is

a comfort—but not a useful tool in
your kit. Same goes for money. Trust your heart?
Risky. You arrived here falling, broken-
winged. Expect scant correlation between
love and safety. Every eighteen minutes—
weighted with stones—someone jumps from a bridge.

Divisible

Head east from California past red
Aztec sandstone in the Valley of Fire,
to the subterranean metal lake
where mined lithium ignited, through
dust-choked miles of twitching livestock.

Head west from New York
through the fruited plains of the rough
Amish—inbred puppies, bent horses,
spent cows—past flickering strip malls
and the Rust Belt's forlorn fortresses.

At the country's midpoint, by the meatpacking
plants of Kansas, those two routes will meet—
remote from both coasts where in faux-rustic
restaurants silver glints, butter glistens, and we
the people—fine diners—await our steaks.

The Boys
    (For Yerra Sugarman)

The day of brave boys is diminished
by blighted night. At home, green summer
closes, golden oaks are over. Soldier

ghosts roam our shaded lanes. All money
is white money. All money is dark
as sick limbs hacked from elms. Spring leaves

will swaddle the wounds and, thank God,
scars will harden. Though we know what's missing,
our eyes still see complete trees. To live

we self-deceive. The boys, do they foresee
the dark, pray God hardens their hearts?
Boys hungry for steady paychecks. Boys who

ditch Flint and Lynchburg to rock the cradle
of civilization. Boys who, killing time,
play old-school card games, scratch

their girls' names in parched
dirt, feed sweets to orphan
dogs. Once none but you, God,

could shock and awe. We at home
call our dogs inside. Driven by wildfire,
coyotes disturb suburban shrubbery,

crash trash cans. We hear fearful
clanging. Are you a phantom
limb, God, known only when gone?

My Little Planet

I pay my daughter to brush my hair.
Frightening are the possibilities of teeth.
Here, have a slice of pie.
We will never live in Haiti.

Cars are islands with native populations.
To know the neighbors, use binoculars.
I am not for every market.
Eclipses always disappoint.

Check the furniture; those children must be somewhere.
The knife comes clean, the cake is done.
No, I didn't cross some frozen tundra.
Play conundrum on a drum.

Darling, your penmanship is execrable.
Recall the war and skin grows moist.
Picture a Mount Rushmore for Women.
Is it too late to train my voice?

How to Arrive at a Motel

Arrive in a swirl of fifties pearls,
toting mother's red leather hatbox,
lips a violet, fists prim in white gloves.

Show up postmarked with poor grades,
low bowling scores, botched dentistry,
your story conceived in a 7-Eleven parking lot.

Or come alone in a rented car with nothing
but the price tag on your sweat suit,
hair fragrant with diner bacon.

Sign your real name. Smile like money.
Know the phone won't ring. Use the pool.
Don't ask how far to the next motel.

The Maréchal de Mouchy Departs a Funeral

After I tire of the cathedral's
distant ceiling and organ's mournful roar
(most of my troops did not survive the war),
after I travel home alone, the coach
cold, whipped horses bloody—I find myself
inclined to consume a brace of pigeons.
Like slumbering lovers, a pretty pair
rests on my plate. How easy to sever

tiny limbs, heads, wings that once touched heaven.
Why does this gentle dismembering soothe
me? I pick warm flesh from sockets with my
thumbnail, teeth, knife. I eat the heart, arise
from the table pleasantly resigned. Let
no part of those little lives be wasted.

Accident

I want to say slow down. You know this dance.
It's late and deer wait to fly over low fences.
Deer gather among black branches.
Behind the trees lie deep woods
and other deer about to leap.

I want to say our headlights are ready to paint
a false gleam in their eyes. Put on your brights.
But as we keep speeding toward the point
where the deer will appear, my lips freeze,
heart opens to what we have not chosen.

After Halloween

Whole blocks haunted by fatigue, the city
sleeps off its sugar high. Stray dogs collapse
in parks. Books lie splayed. Computers shoot blue
light. Candles die, pumpkins go dark. Paper
skeletons twitch, might be alive. Midnight
the time changes. People neglect to reset
clocks. Devil mask swings on gate. Feverish,
real estate prices rise. Alarms strike late.

On a stalled subway, the night shift adrift:
nurse, bouncer, runaway. Could be the start
of a joke. It's not. Above ground we pray:
May daybreak hobble goblins. Forgive us
our fun. Let us forget that which kills us
rests in our bodies till it manifests.

Burnt Orchard

Centuries ago
the apple trees
up in flames.

Last August
a freak blaze—
our barn lost.

Lightning strike,
human error,
or wires frayed?

We don't know
when the familiar
will again ignite.

Yesterday you gathered
brittle branches, remains
of a sweet season.

You stood the bundled wood
in the open field
that once was orchard.

Thanksgiving we'll spark
a bonfire—light we've willed
shattering the black sky.

Another Art

It's always dusk in the sonogram room.
On the screen glow tornadoes. Like the cold
gel she squeezes over your abdomen,
the technician will eventually
warm to the wreck that is your body—no
spleen, no breasts, a chunk of lung gone. Now this
mystery lump. You lie back. The thick wand works
dark magic, explores your mortal torso.

Breathe, she gently repeats. On your side, please.
Facing away, you are a masterpiece.
Ingres odalisque, Stradivarius
cello. Exquisite the dip between rib
and hip. Your blue robe falls open, the tie
dangling in twilight. You, a life study.

Next

By the time you read this, the half-full
water glass on the desk: evaporated.
The gravel drive crushed to a thin line
in geology's story. My vintage milk bottles
(We come to visit, not to stay. Return to dairy every day!)
sold at a yard sale—along with the clay fly
from a friend who died young, the cake
knife that traveled from Riga.

Gone, my handprints from kitchen
cabinets. Ditto the dog's saliva
from porch doors. Bitterweed I fought
now another woman's trouble.
May she admire October's
mellow light, feel Orion alert
in the ancient sky, see magnolias
explode above the dirt road.

Revival
(New York City, 2002)

Snakes sprout from severed heads,
and one stone serpent's tongue
doubles as a sacrificial knife.

Fertility and rebirth states our blithe
museum guide. She's that age
where nothing's terminal.

We all wonder about the weapon—
how quickly it slips from the serpent's jaws,
when last used, on whom.

Drought, dust, global roast.
I haven't known lust in months.
My own sharp tongue has destroyed plenty.

Today on the subway a girl's eyes
shut like a doll's. A man cradled
an empty crate. Wheels squealed.

Quietly we occupied our territories.
When the sign flashed *3:08 p.m. 86th Street*
I thought *This is humanity's finest hour.*

II.

Oh

The amusing serpent twisted
into an O. That apple sweet as her

slowly sighed Oh—mouth open
around the smooth fruit she thought

holy. No. Her moans sonorous.
A strange taste invaded her. Oh

woeful boldness! Over in a moment.
Then does she know the world no

longer whole. A hole opened.
Those who lived and locomoted

no longer spoke. Lonely and
clothed, she felt the world fold.

All she'd let go now choked, closed.
So cold after the afterglow. Oh.

Bed

While making the bed,
a déjà vu of making the bed.

Love is a different kind of making,
though it too transpires in bed.

Sometimes I think why bother. It will
only get messed up again—the bed.

We leapt the garden gate,
slept late in a marigold bed.

Unlike love that misleads, these letters
make the shape of what they mean—*bed*.

Leaving you would be easy (that's untrue)
as throwing a clean sheet over the bed.

They have in common lying—
your untrusty love and a bed.

Once dashing active verb,
now dull noun—*bed*.

Drunk on wine or fresh love, could
we yet float this sobered bed?

Bodice Ripper

I found you in the veins of love. Your soft,
soft cheeks plump as riverbanks in flood time.
Stunned as a dove dumbstruck by thorns, my love,
I loved you the way bloodletting begets
betterness. Rose-violet before—now more
scarlet than cardinals adrift in snowdrifts.
Disarmed am I by your white, white arms—oh
gardens of gardenias. Our battle done.

We both have won. Fluid as youth, our hearts
and arteries. Compulsive, my wordless
iambs pulse. Your robbery translates my
mouth. In breakage and spillage, I take you
to be my pillager. Who writes like this
anymore? My thighs—tender tinder—ignite.

You Can Know How to Swim & Still Drown

I've been unmoored by his kind before, you see.
Hot nights permit dips in starlit seas.

At gas stations, pharmacies, groceries.
Each outgoing current greets incoming sea.

Eyes meet at the register, voraciously.
This dictum holds: bathe not alone at sea.

I notice what he's chosen to imbibe or eat.
Narrow is the range for comfortable seas.

Then disregard the Red Bull and Dexedrine.
Blue lips and clammy skin mean one should cease.

In icy retail climates, I crave heat.
Most springtime drownings are due to frigid seas.

The air's conditioned, but to what?—quips he.
Even strong swimmers flail in rough seas.

Such an original mind!—I flatter, then propose we flee.
When light strikes ocean, one cannot see.

Let's take this to a bar—he laughs, agrees.
Pleasure unduly prolongs time undersea.

My body's mainly wine—I wink, guzzling Burgundy.
If one is caught in seaweed, the heart may seize.

Mrs. Sherlock Holmes States Her Case

Milk-chocolate sweeties sour his breath.
Tiny bubbles rise from his teeth
in their bedside tumbler.
His conversation's a soggy crumpet.
And don't get him started on the Pakistanis.
He adores Mum, Brighton in August,
sea awash with sewage, too cold to swim,
hotel brimming with red-faced widows.
Après bingo, their love moans fade the wallpaper.

A thick-skulled child, he spent days with birds,
binoculars slung from his ostrich neck,
shock of albino ankle above sagging socks,
fingers cradling a robin
sling-shot by someone smarter.

How can I get anything done?
Dog-faced Watson curled on the rug,
basset eyes fixed on my husband.
I think it's love. The fire dying,
both of them too lazy to stoke it.
Can't they pick themselves up,
solve something: Jack the Ripper,
hounds on the moors, whatever.
Back by dinner, boots caked with dung,
fox-death. Heads in ether.
And those moth-food tweeds!
That damn hat! That pipe stench!
That magnifying glass he wouldn't need
were he not too vain for glasses.
And that stomach rash, what is it?

There's a war on. Science needs advancing.
But he's caught up in two-bit mysteries.
Let him unclog the kitchen drain,
put the children to bed
if he can remember their names,
our boys barefoot while he's shod
in Bond Street's bench-made best,
baffled I'm still here.

House of Smoke

Smoke soaked mother's mink stole. Tobacco trumped
her Chanel No. 5, flecked *Playboys* stashed
in father's bureau. Lucky Strike, Old Gold
fumes caressed the sunroom sofa where she
breakfasted on black coffee and tunneled
up from night. Sundays smoke floated over
cherry soup, prime rib, Grand Marnier soufflé.
Smoke perfumed my parents' bleached, ironed sheets,
fogged the Venetian glass mirror. Matching
packs of Pall Malls bedecked the bed tables.
Ashtrays overflowed when lipsticked mother
paced (blouse printed with forget-me-nots) while
awaiting father, so-called working late—
and when (later, divorced) she primped for dates.

High Dive

My entire nine years
are prelude to this climb
higher than a house.
Halfway up the chrome ladder,
I kiss the known world goodbye:
the shallow end, cosseted children,
lifeguard's glistening whistle,
my mother, my brother.
Forehead jeweled with sweat,
I test the edge,
fathom I am alone. Then—
aching to arc—I leap.
My molecules sing,
bones know:
never was a girl so great,
never was fear
more vanquished
in the history
of the Americana Hotel.

The Lovers

See how blithely she rests her hand on his
knee while she navigates, he drives. How they
walk lockstep without trying. How they post
notes on their refrigerator for all
to view: *My real life began the day I
met you.* At restaurants they order in
tandem, wordlessly exchange plates halfway
through each course. They have never spent a night

apart. Is it beautiful? Or is it
terrifying, wonder those of us who
get by on less. Somewhere in the deep, calm
pond of their love, surely they know (unlike
swans who also mate for life) that one of
them will vanish before the other.

Ferns, Lichens, Liverworts, etc.

Despair is everywhere between the lines
of *The Oxford Book of Flowerless Plants*.
Unequipped to demand attention, those
homely flora live tiny lives. To what
purpose their photosynthesis? From all
possible light, they gain only width, height.
Their greens darken, deepen. Some spend their days
concealing concrete foundations, battling
crabgrass. Some serve as neutral backdrop for
seductive blossoms flaunted by others.
The meek are doomed to usefulness, not joy.
No miraculous transformations—no
thrill of stamen and pistil, no bursting
open as zinnia, morning glory.

Courtship Behavior of the Alligator

Macerating in muck or the godforsaken Saint
Augustine Alligator Farm Lake, for God's sake,

they display radiance, grace. Jaws that can mash
bone slacken with passion. The female waddles,

straddles the male. They groove through ooze, mud
studded with tiny shining flies. His baritone moans

create aqueous vibrations. His tail flails. She opens wide,
her teeth swamp-diamonds. What woman wouldn't smile?

Transmuted by their ardor, I do. As if sluiced into
a juicy Eden I once knew, as if scales embellished

my flesh, as if I nuzzled the male's muzzle,
I sigh. Oh viscous delicious! Oh thigh vise!

All Vermeer

We are all Vermeer.
What I mean is sit by this window.
Write. There's still time.
No end to invented light.
Those cherries are your ticket.
That frozen lake. Listen.
As hours kill, chimes make fireworks.
Even though six state birds
have flown the coop,
Pluto turns out to be a moon,
and the new ballyhooed cure
a fake. Even if your mirror's
a dead end and rumors
about the human animal are true.
Make no mistake. Even then
you are Vermeer.

The Button Master's Apprentice

> *All the more I wish to see*
> *in those blossoms at dawn*
> *the face of the god*
>   —Basho

If, drawing thread through cloth,
I could return the needle to the exact
place eight times without leaving a hole.
If I could make from wood or shells or clay
buttons smooth or rough and pleasing
to touch. If I could fit the little disk or knob
or sphere to its allotted slot so it held
but did not lock, was loose without droop.
If I knew how to choose buttons—brass
acorns or glass hearts—for the shirt
or skirt or suit. If I could sight-read
centimeters, precisely slit buttonholes
with one swift stroke—needling perfect
circles through air to secure the edges,
tugging each stitch tight. If the edges
never unraveled, if I could align
three rows of buttons on a sleeve,
might I find your smile?

Light

You turn New Jersey Siberian blue
without you moons would starve
sketcher of parallelograms on cubicle desks
spinner of nets across still pools
infrared visible ultraviolet X
raiser of spirits
you fade newspapers feed leaves
bleacher of fish skulls and beach towels
headdress for the holy
punctuator of yellow plates

O most electromagnetic radiator
witness to our beauty and failures
we read you with feeble meters
you who strike us at birth
insistent visitor ender of mysteries
daily bread sign of warm bed
and someone home

In Case You Misunderstood

If the causes cause unsolicited reasons
for you to return I won't question your absence,
because your fluid beauty could fill the moon's dry
seas (Mare Serenitatis, Mare Tranquillitatis, Mare Humorum)
with bright life (Yellowtail Damselfish, White Grunts,
Red Hinds). So you see the mistakes. Some say
grace. Something from tribulation. When I called you
Euphorbia Tirucalli, I meant Pencil Tree. When I whispered
Ficus Lyrata, I meant Banjo Fig. Persea Americana is
Alligator Pear, I swear. And should you murmur
Pisonia Subcordata, I'll hear Water Mampoo.
How many peaks you can make if I use all
the power of my country! Like that, I love you.

Acknowledgments

Grateful acknowledgment is made to the publications in which the following poems first appeared:

Epoch: "Revival"

Mudfish: "Geography"

Open City: "How to Arrive at a Motel"; "Mrs. Sherlock Holmes States Her Case"

Phoebe: "All Vermeer"

Poet Lore: "High Dive"

Running with Water: "Next"; "The Lovers"

The Massachusetts Review: "Light"; "Welcome to Guardian Angel School"

The Saint Ann's Review: "Another Art"

The South Carolina Review: "Bed"

The Spoon River Poetry Review: "Accident"

With Thanks

The enthusiasm, wisdom, and generosity of many people (and a few dogs) have made these poems possible. You have my deepest gratitude.

My work has been immeasurably improved by the astute comments of writing groups: Jordan Franklin, Natalya Sukhonos, and Denise Utt; Jackie Gavron, Abigail Hastings, and Iris Rosenberg; Susan Buttenwieser, Jennifer Cooke, and Alice Naude.

The MacDowell Colony and the Virginia Center for the Creative Arts have provided invaluable time and space.

Exemplary poet/teachers who have encouraged and enlightened me include Grace Bonner, Billy Collins, Marilyn Hacker, John Frederick Nims, Rowan Ricardo Phillips, Julie Sheehan, and Mark Strand.

Céline Keating has been my dear mentor for the writing life. I am grateful to Tom and Celia Sonnabend for their steady presence and quirky humor. And to Dalia Gold for casting light.

Thanks to Susan Becher, Betty Branda, Alice Dalton Brown, Ferris Cook, Patricia Feiwel, Giggie Heine, Peggy Maisel, Anita Merk, Margaret Mintz, Cherrie Nanninga, Ann Schaumburger, Susie Shaffer, Dena Sneider, Helen Taylor, and Alicia Whitaker for your enduring, extraordinary friendship. Thanks to Candice Odell and Julian Shapiro, Renee Edison and Don Kaplan, and Gloria and David Gerstein for walks and talks. Thanks to Nancy Alexander and Rob Steinberg for extending my family.

Always in my heart are my parents Norma and Irving Winer, and the bright spirits of Arch Garland III and Jennifer Lewis.

Thank you, Leah Maines, for choosing my manuscript as the winner of this Finishing Line Press Open Chapbook Competition.

Jody Winer is a fellow of the MacDowell Colony and the Virginia Center for the Creative Arts. Her poems have appeared in *Epoch, The Massachusetts Review, Open City, Phoebe, Poet Lore, The South Carolina Review, The Spoon River Poetry Review, The Atlanta Review,* and other journals. She has worked as a librarian, writer, and dog wrangler. She holds an MA from the University of Kent, Canterbury, England; an MLS from Simmons College; and a BA from Pomona College—and was a Trustee Scholar at the University of Chicago. Raised in Florida, she lives in New York.

www.ingramcontent.com/pod-product-compliance
Lightning Source LLC
LaVergne TN
LVHW041559070426
835507LV00011B/1177